A NATIONAL TRUST POCKET BOOK

BIRDS

OF THE COAST

by REG JONES

INTRODUCTION

The coast is the meeting place of the sea and the land. Since the sea is tidal, the constant ebb and flow of water exposes wet areas of sand, mud and rock twice a day which, because of their very wetness, are rich in marine life such as seaweeds, snails and worms. This same marine life in turn represents the food of other animals, particularly birds, and there are few other places where birds can be seen feeding in such numbers. But the coast has another part to play. Some birds spend most of their lives quartering the oceans far from land obtaining their food by fishing. Of necessity, they must come ashore to lay their eggs and rear their chicks and the majority take up temporary residence on those parts of the coast which offer a safe sanctuary, often assembling in considerable numbers. Many such species show a tendency to nest in close association with their own kind, their colonies being memorable sights.

The nature of the coast varies. There are stretches of rocky cliffs, often sheer and precipitous, while in contrast there are flatter shores with spacious sand and mud flats backed by dunes and salt marshes. Each habitat has something to offer and since birds vary in their requirements different species are found populating particular areas

Lofty cliffs plunging almost vertically into the water and with no loose rocks at sea-level obviously offer practically nothing in the way of food to birds. However, if the rock face is faulted, creating ledges and crevices, these may be occupied as nesting sites by seabirds. Kittiwakes cement cup-like nests on the slightest rocky projections providing there is scope for a tightly organised communal group to be established. Fulmars need larger platforms, often with some overhead cover, and they will tolerate quite wide separation from their neighbours. They are often found on cliffs composed of relatively soft material where cavities of appreciable size may develop. In addition they demonstrate less rigidity in their choice of site, sometimes breeding on steep rather than sheer slopes. To some extent the gannet is similar, occupying spacious flat ledges on cliffs at all levels while, at the same time, colonies may spill over cliff brows on to adjacent gentle slopes. Horizontal ledges are much favoured by guillemots, the birds standing in close formations, laying their eggs on the bare rock. Where

Opposite top, kittiwakes; **opposite bottom,** gannet

Guillemots on top of a rocky stack

isolated stacks rise from the sea, their flat tops may be densely populated. Razorbills, on the other hand, prefer not to incubate their eggs in the open, usually retreating into fissures or beneath loose rocks. In somewhat similar fashion the puffin hides its egg, most frequently in a burrow in the turf near a cliff top or on an island. Another seabird likely to be seen on sheer cliffs is the shag, which builds bulky nests on narrow platforms at various levels. Sometimes they are in the splash zone or in semi-darkness in a sea cave. In contrast, the very similar cormorant prefers more spacious quarters and is more usually found on open terraces, often on offshore stacks.

Herring gull nesting among loose rocks

On the mainland, cliffs must be extremely steep if they are to provide real protection for nesting birds but on islands, where there is less chance of interference, more gradual inclines may be used as breeding sites. Rock-strewn slopes often harbour nesting gulls: colonies of herring gulls on the upper slopes with lesser black-backed gulls on the flatter ground above. Great black-backed gulls nest here and there on rocky prominences. They are predators on smaller species including those that burrow such as Manx shearwaters and puffins. At sea-level, where there are loose rocks, marine life flourishes and at low tide some birds will forage for food. This group will include the oystercatcher, turnstone and purple sandpiper, each one being adept at dealing with the creatures encountered on a rocky shore. Of the three, only the oystercatcher will lay its eggs on the pebbly strand above the high water mark. If, in such situations, there are piles of boulders with hidden tunnels and cavities, then, in northern Britain, black guillemots may take advantage of the cover for breeding.

Oystercatcher, a long-billed wader

Low-lying coasts present a very different picture. Where shallow bays face the open sea, spacious sandy flats are exposed by the ebbing tide. At first sight they may appear barren and sterile but in the lower part of the shore where the surface of the sand is ridged and wet there is evidence of life. One indicator is the presence of coiled threads of sand which are the casts of lugworms. These have the ability to burrow thus escaping the effects of dessication when the sand is not covered by the sea. Dwellers on a sandy shore must be capable of retreating beneath the surface at low tide. Apart from lugworms, there are cockles, bristle worms and more static tube-forming worms. Consequently, any bird feeding on a sandy shore must be able to reach this hidden prey and only the long-billed waders, notably the oystercatcher, are adequately equipped. In addition, gulls may forage amongst the tidal litter and parties of sanderlings often scurry along the water's edge investigating what is brought ashore by each successive wave.

Colony (ternery) of Sandwich terns

Dune systems often develop on the landward side of open sandy beaches. Blown sand accumulates forming embryonic dunes which are stabilized by such plants as marram grass, the branching underground parts binding together the loose material. Over the years the dunes may become extensive with the older and more mature dunes having many attractive plants and a fauna which includes a variety of insects. Small birds such as meadow pipits, skylarks and wheatears may breed and, where there is little disturbance, colonies of seabirds may be established including those of several species of gulls and terns. Each colony will have its characteristic features. Common terns' nests may be quite widely separated whereas sandwich terns breed in closely packed groups and are often associated with black-headed gulls. Sand dunes may also harbour other species whose nests are scattered here and there. Shelducks lay their eggs in rabbit burrows while redshanks hide their clutches within tufts of marram. Occasionally, a short-eared owl may take up residence.

Mud flat, feeding ground of waders

While there is an appreciable amount of life to be found on a sandy shore, it cannot match that which flourishes in the mud flats which are a feature of broad shallow estuaries and sheltered creeks. In such situations fine particles of silt brought down by the rivers settle out and, mixing with any underlying sand, form a nutritious mud which may be further enriched by material brought in from the sea. On the surface eel-grass, sea lettuce and the green filamentous seaweed *Enteromorpha* grow, but it is within the mud itself that life really abounds. Sometimes the surface appears almost granular due to the abundance of the tiny snail, the laver spire shell, *Hydrobia ulvae*. Little more than half a centimetre in length, its numbers may reach 50,000 to the square metre. It browses on weed and also on the microscopic life in the mud. Being capable of existing in varying degrees of salinity, it can penetrate estuaries and this ability is also possessed by other mud flat dwellers such as the sand-hopper *Corophium volutator*, which lives in fine tubes in the upper muddy layers. It, too, can be very numerous with several thousand to the square metre. Of the larger animals, the cockle may be present, but not in the same numbers as in clean sand. But there are other bi-valves

Laver spire shell

Baltic tellin

Cockle

Ragworm

Items of food found in mud

snails such as the Baltic tellin, *Macoma balthica*, and the sand gaper, *Mya arenaria*, which lies very deep in the mud. Lugworms may also occur where sand still predominates, disappearing in softer muds where, however, there are other bristle worms like the ragworm, *Nereis diversicolor*, which is an active burrower. Thus there is life at a number of levels and different birds exploit the various possibilities. Some ducks and geese feed on the weed. A local name for eel-grass is wigeon-grass. Shelducks take large quantities of the surface-dwelling snail, *Hydrobia ulvae*, but it is the waders, with their variously shaped bills, which are best equipped to harvest the creatures within the mud. Short-billed plovers concentrate on the surface. Knots, with more extended bills, take large numbers of Baltic tellins lying a few centimetres deep. Redshanks take surface dwellers, including many *Corophia* together with worms and snails from lower layers while long-billed godwits and curlews probe even deeper to reach their prey.

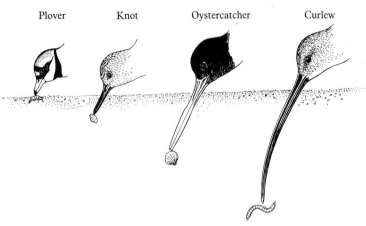

Plover Knot Oystercatcher Curlew

Specialised bills of waders

Estuarine mud flats play host to large numbers of waders. At peak times, more than a quarter of a million birds may be seen in Morecambe Bay, while the Ribble estuary, the Wash and the Solway Firth may attract almost as many.

As silt accumulates in shallow sheltered waters, the floor rises and, as a result, the muddy margins are exposed to the air for increasing lengths of time during each tidal cycle. In due course a salt marsh develops. Initially, one or two plants, marsh samphire and annual sea blite, colonise the mud. Both can exist in salty conditions and their presence inhibits the free movement of water, thus accelerating the deposition of more silt and the gradual establishment of firmer ground. Typical salt marsh plants now appear: sea lavender, sea aster and sea purslane. The marsh may still be covered by the highest tides, water draining away along sinuous channels or runnels.

Salt marsh plants offer little in the way of food to the larger birds although their seeds may be eaten by pipits, buntings and finches. Waders may feed in the muddy bottoms of the runnels and along the watery fringes. Any nests built on a salt marsh are at risk, often being washed out by a tidal surge. However, if some reclamation has taken place creating 'fresh' grassy marshes, these may offer safe breeding stations for such species as the redshank.

Shingle beaches are a feature of some coastlines. Banks or ridges of pebbles are built by waves breaking on the shore at an angle, rolling pebbles upwards. Often such a ridge will extend outwards as a spit across the mouth of a river, deflecting its course so that for a time water flows between the spit and the land before reaching the open sea. Where shallow rivers are flanked by salt marshes these will lie sheltered, between the mainland and the shingle spit. Shingle banks are not hospitable habitats. There is very little marine life although a few plants such as sea campion and yellow horned poppy may be established on the landward, and more sheltered, side. Thus, apart from seeds, there is no food for coastal birds but a few may nest. They include oystercatchers and ringed plovers together with some terns, especially the little tern.

Little tern nesting on shingle

PETRELS AND SHEARWATERS Family: Procellariidae

This is one family of seabirds within the Order Procellariiformes. These are tube-nosed birds in which the opening of the nostrils is at the end of a tube extending along the upper half of the bill, the surface of which is covered with horny plates. Their wings are long and narrow, features of birds which are adept at gliding. The term 'shearwatering' refers to a type of gliding flight so close to the water that with each change of direction the stiffly outstretched wings appear to cleave the surface. Except when they are breeding, petrels and shearwaters spend all their lives ranging the oceans feeding on small animals associated with the plankton in the upper layers. They breed in colonies with some smaller species nesting out of sight in burrows; single-egg clutches are laid. When brooding, birds are often noisy, producing a variety of sounds including bubbling cackles and more guttural calls. If a bird is disturbed by an intruder an offensive oil is forcibly discharged from the mouth as a deterrent.

Fulmar in flight

Fulmar at rest

Fulmar *Fulmarus glacialis* 47cm

Fulmars are oceanic birds confined to the northern hemisphere. They range widely over the North Atlantic, penetrating deep into the Arctic wherever there is open water. Prior to 1878 no fulmars nested in Britain apart from a colony on St Kilda. Since that time there has been a remarkable increase in the range and the numbers of the species and birds can now be seen at almost all suitable nesting sites around the British coastline. The reason for this development is not absolutely clear. While the natural food of the fulmar probably consists of items taken from the surface plankton, it also takes oily blubber and its success in modern times may have been assisted by the commercial development of deep-sea fishing. Fishing fleets are accompanied far from land by flocks of fulmars waiting for offal which is often discarded before freshly-caught fish is stored in ice. This freely available source of nourishment may well have been a major factor promoting the development of the population. It has also been suggested that within the original groups some birds developed an urge to break away and disperse, a phenomenon well illustrated in other species.

Fulmars may appear at their breeding stations as early as November, the sites being broad cliff ledges, spaces between rocks, or the corners of deserted buildings on remote islands. Here they begin to display. Two birds sitting together, and sometimes accompanied by a third, stretch their necks upwards and swing them from side to side with their mouths wide open emitting a guttural 'ag-ag-ag-ag-ag-ag-arr'. They subside into silence and then suddenly the ritual is repeated. When not squatting on a ledge or boulder a fulmar glides effortlessly to and fro along the face of a cliff on stiffly extended wings, turning and banking at the end of each beat. Although gull-like in form the wings are narrower and they lack black tips, while the neck is shorter as is the bill which bears the prominent tubular nostrils. There is some variation in plumage. Normally the head, neck and underparts are white with a yellowish tinge, the back and wings being pearl-grey. A small proportion are completely grey and are said to belong to a dark phase. Such birds are more numerous in groups situated further north.

Manx Shearwater *Puffinus puffinus* 36cm

As with other petrels and shearwaters, the Manx shearwater spends the autumn and winter at sea, many being present off the east coast of South America. At sea it glides on long narrow wings close to the water, tilting from side to side as the waves roll beneath it. Since the bird is black above and white below such rocking movements give the impression of a black and white flicker. It feeds on small fish taken from the surface or during shallow dives.

In spring and summer flocks or 'rafts' of shearwaters assemble each evening on the sea close inshore near to their breeding sites. Being rather helpless on the ground they do not fly inland until about two hours after sunset, thus escaping the attentions of marauding gulls. Each pair excavates a burrow and incubation is carried out by both parents with an interval of several days separating each change-over. During the day there is no sight or sound of a bird above ground but a

Manx shearwater

ight there is a complete transformation. Sitting birds cackle and
roon in their burrows to be answered by those flying above. Birds
umble out of the sky and, their legs lacking the strength to fully
upport their bodies, they fall forward to rest on their bellies. Young
hearwaters remain underground for about ten weeks whereupon,
aving been deserted by their parents, they scramble to the sea in
larkness and move relatively quickly to their wintering areas. They
vill not return to European waters until they are two years old and are
aid not to breed before they are five.

The largest colonies are found on islands off the west coast such as
kokholm and Skomer, the greatest number being on Rhum where
ver 100,000 pairs breed. Smaller groups use mainland cliffs, again in
he west.

Storm petrel

STORM PETRELS Family: Hydrobatidae

These are small tube-nosed seabirds, many of them not much larger than sparrows, which are darkly coloured but often show some areas of whiteness. Their legs are very slender with webbed feet and are almost useless on land, which is only visited when breeding and then at night. Their flight is erratic and fluttering with their feet pattering on the water as morsels of food are snatched from the plankton. Occasionally they may alight briefly and dip under the surface.

Storm petrels lay single-egg clutches which are hidden in rock crevices or in burrows. Their presence can sometimes be inferred by the musky smell usually associated with the birds or by the crooning song of a resident bird. Like shearwaters, they may vomit oil if they are disturbed.

Storm Petrel *Hydrobates pelagicus* 15cm

This species is the smallest of European seabirds. Although it is largely dark in colour there is whiteness on the rump above the square black tail and also at the base of the underwing. In addition a faint light wing bar can be seen on the upper surface of the wing. The breeding biology is similar to that of the Manx shearwater but nocturnal visits to land occur as soon as it is dark and moonlight is no eterrent. On alighting they do not linger for long on the ground before entering their nesting chambers. They are not at home on land, supporting themselves on the full length of the tarsus, shuffling and fluttering awkwardly.

Because of their habits the presence of breeding storm petrels may be difficult to establish and the estimation of numbers even more so. Nevertheless they are probably numerous with colonies occurring on remote islands lying off the west coast from the Scillies to the Shetlands. After breeding they move away, one wintering area being in South African waters.

The status of a second species, Leach's Petrel, *Oceanodroma leucorhoa* (20cm), is more obscure. In Britain it is known to breed on a very few islands off northern Scotland. Larger and longer-winged than the storm petrel, it has a forked tail, but is usually recognised by its non-stop fluttering flight close to the water.

left, storm petrel; **right,** Leach's petrel

GANNETS Family: Sulidae

The gannets, together with the boobies found in tropical waters, are *family of powerful seabirds with long pointed wings and bodies whic* *because of the long dagger-like bills and extended wedge-shaped tai* *appear to taper at each end. They fly with regular wing-beats punctuate* *by occasional glides. Food is obtained by diving from heights of up to thirt* *metres, their prey, usually fish or squid, being snatched rather tha* *speared and swallowed as they surface. Their strong bodies are capable c* *withstanding the impact of a dive and the forward-looking eyes, togethe* *with absence of open nostrils on the bill, are advantageous.*

Gannets breed on deserted islands or on inaccessible cliff ledges. A singl *egg is laid in a rough nest of seaweed and flotsam and incubated in* *curious way. Most birds have brood patches where eggs come into direc* *contact with the warm skin of the parent. A gannet has no brood patc* *and instead covers the egg carefully with its feet before sitting. Adult bird* *are predominantly white in colour with the tips of the wings, an* *sometimes the tail, dark. Juveniles are dark above with white speckles* *lighter underneath with brownish markings. They only achieve adul* *plumage after several moults, becoming lighter in a series of stages.*

Gannet *Sula bassana* 90cm

The gannet is Britain's largest seabird with a wingspan of almost two metres. It breeds on both sides of the North Atlantic, approximately seventy per cent of the population nesting round Britain and Ireland in gannetries, many of which have been established for centuries. The largest is on St Kilda but colonies of several thousand pairs are present on the more accessible Bass Rock, Ailsa Craig and Grassholm. Smaller groups, more recent in origin can be seen on Bempton Cliffs in Yorkshire and on Scar Rocks off the south-west Scottish coast.

Birds arrive at their breeding stations early in the year but, incubation and fledging being lengthy, gannetries are occupied until early autumn. Young birds, which have been reared on regurgitated food, migrate in their first winter as far as the coast of West Africa. They will not breed until they are five or six years old at which time, after nesting, the urge to move southwards is diminished and they disperse within European waters.

Opposite, gannet

Cormorants nesting on broad rocky shelf

CORMORANTS Family: Phalacrocoracidae

These are large birds which are largely black in colour, the feather frequently possessing a metallic sheen. The eyes, the bill and parts of the face may be more brightly marked. In addition, when in breeding dress birds often develop crests and similar plumed adornments. In form, a long sinuous neck joins an elongated body which terminates in a stiff fan shaped tail. Usually they fly close to the water with their necks outstretched, their broad wings beating steadily in flapping flight Cormorants are expert divers, the body normally springing from the surface in an arc as the bird submerges. Fish and crustaceans are their main prey and these are secured by their slim, almost cylindrical bills which are sharply hooked. When they are not fishing they soon leave the water and, on landing, adopt a spread-eagle pose to dry off their feathers which appear to be less efficiently waterproofed than those of other diving birds.

Cormorants breed in colonies, building nests of seaweed and other available material on rocky islets, cliff ledges or in trees. The young are orn naked, but soon acquire a downy covering which is replaced by uvenile plumage, usually dark brown in colour.

Cormorant *Phalacrocorax carbo* 90cm

The cormorant is found in shallow coastal waters, especially in sheltered bays and estuaries. It is a bottom feeder, taking numbers of flat-fish. In addition it often appears inland on lakes and rivers where it may catch a variety of fish including eels and trout.

A cormorant's dark plumage has a bronze cast. The bill is yellow, the chin and cheeks are white. In spring there is a light mark on the thigh which is conspicuous in flight and, while the head does not bear a crest, the feathers at the back are somewhat elongated thus creating a thickened band or mane. Immature birds are distinguished by having the lower breast and belly dull white. These features are readily seen as they stand with wings outstretched when drying off.

When breeding, colonies are usually sited on more or less flat ground which may be a broad shelf near the base of a cliff or the top of an islet. Such situations are normally associated with rocky coasts. Sometimes, at inland stations, nests are built in trees; this no longer occurs in Britain although there are tree-nesting communities in Ireland and on the Continent. After breeding there is some dispersal, mainly southwards, with most birds returning the following spring to the colony where they were hatched.

Shag or Green Cormorant *Phalacrocorax aristotelis* 76cm

The shag, like the cormorant, is found in coastal waters but it does not venture inland. It dives in deeper water catching free-swimming fish, sand-eels and sprats which make up a large part of its diet. It is sometimes called the 'green cormorant' because of the green iridescence on the plumage. In adult birds the angle of the jaw is bright yellow and at the start of the breeding season both sexes possess distinctive upturned crests.

The nests are built on narrow cliff ledges or in the spaces between boulders on very rocky ground. Occasionally they are hidden in sea caves or lodged within narrow gullies. Older birds acquire the more sheltered sites thus deriving more protection from heavy spray which may chill the young. Not surprisingly, colonies are usually restricted to more rocky coasts. On leaving the nest the young are buffish brown,

becoming darker at the end of their first year. In contrast to youn,
cormorants they do not show large areas of whiteness on their bellies
In the autumn there is some dispersal with birds tending to reappea
the following year at the place where they were hatched.

Shag, or green cormorant

SWANS, GEESE AND DUCKS Family: Anatidae

These are aquatic birds, the three front toes being connected by a web to assist with swimming. They float buoyantly, having water-repellant plumage and a rich covering of down. Except for those ducks known as 'sawbills', their bills are flattened, the tip being covered by a horny plate called the 'nail' and the edges bear rows of fine projections which help in obtaining a grip on slippery water plants. When airborne, they fly with necks outstretched, their wings being long and pointed with eleven primary flight feathers which are moulted simultaneously each year. At this time the birds are flightless for a few weeks.

The family is divided into two sub-families.

SWANS AND GEESE Sub-family Anserinae.

These are usually larger and longer necked than ducks; the sexes are similar in appearance and the male plays a part in family life, standing guard near the sitting female and helping to tend the young.

Swans are the largest of the waterfowl and those found in the northern hemisphere are predominantly white, the juveniles being grey and becoming lighter as they grow older. They do not breed successfully until they are three or four years old.

Geese are confined to the northern hemisphere. They are rather smaller than swans, with somewhat shorter and stubbier bills, the majority obtaining their food by grazing on land. Being gregarious, large flocks are formed in winter. The different species may be divided into two groups, grey geese and black geese.

DUCKS Sub-family Anatinae

Ducks are smaller and shorter-necked than swans and geese; their wings are narrower and beat faster in flight. The males, or drakes, normally take no part in rearing the young. They are often brightly coloured whereas their mates, the ducks, are dressed in subtle patterns of browns and fawns. This is because the ducks must be as unobtrusive as possible when incubating eggs in the open. This duller type of plumage is often assumed by the drakes when, after the summer moult, they are flightless for a short time. A second moult later in the year restores their breeding dress. In many species secondary feathers on the wing are highly coloured, often glinting with a metallic sheen, forming a conspicuous patch or 'speculum'. The sub-family is divided into a number of groups or 'tribes'.

Mute swans

Mute Swan *Cygnus olor* 150cm
Whooper Swan *Cygnus cygnus* 150cm
Bewick's Swan *Cygnus columbianus* 120cm

The mute swan is the commonest and most widely distributed of European swans. It is distinguished by an orange bill which is overhung at the base by a black knob. The neck is normally held in a graceful curve and the wings are arched over the back while the body ends in an upturned tail. Although usually associated with fresh-water habitats some birds may be seen in the upper reaches of estuaries and on sheltered tidal waters.

The whooper swan is a winter visitor from Iceland. It is about the same size as a mute swan but lighter in build and on the water the neck is held erect, the wings are closely applied to the body and the tail is not upturned. At close quarters the bill is black-tipped with a wedge of yellow extending from the base to beyond the nostrils. Flocks appear in winter on estuaries feeding, frequently by up-ending, on aquatic vegetation but they often come ashore to graze on grassland and to explore cultivated land for potatoes and grain.

Bewick's swans resemble whoopers but are smaller and more compact. Their heads are rounder with a suggestion of a forehead and the patch of yellow on the bill is not as extensive as it ends bluntly below the nostril. They are winter visitors from Arctic Russia, feeding for the most part on wet pastures not far from the coast, often flying at dusk to roost on mud flats.

Above, Bewick's swan; **below,** Whooper swan

Pink-footed Goose *Anser brachyrhyncus* 67-76cm
White-fronted Goose *Anser albifrons* 66-76cm
Greylag Goose *Anser anser* 76-89cm

These are grey geese, some of which use coastal roosts on mudflats and sandbanks from where they fly to their feeding grounds.

The pink-footed goose breeds in eastern Greenland, Iceland and Spitsbergen. It is distinguished by its dark head with a pink and black bill and pinkish legs. It is very gregarious and in autumn large flocks from Spitsbergen move through Scandinavia to the eastern seaboard of the North Sea while others from Iceland and Greenland visit Britain, many remaining in central and eastern Scotland with some passing on into northern and eastern England. Estuarine sites which attract them include the Ythan, the Solway Firth, the Ribble and the Wash. On arrival they tend to feed in the stubbles on spilled grain and also on waste potatoes. As the winter progresses the diet changes and by spring they are taking more grass, often enjoying the nutritious early growth on coastal marshes.

The white-fronted goose breeds on the tundra bordering the Arctic coasts of Russia and North America, with a small population in Greenland. There are at least four races, two being winter visitors to Europe. That from Greenland, the orange-billed *A.a.flavirostris*, occurs in Ireland and Scotland while members of the pink-billed Russian race migrate southwards reaching Germany, the Netherlands and eastern and southern Britain. They are in cackling flocks, dropping out of the sky on to grassy feeding grounds such as coastal marshland. They are darker than most other grey geese and the adults show a frontal patch of white on the forehead together with irregular dark bars on the lower breast and belly, features which are absent from first winter birds.

The greylag goose is more heavily built than other grey geese, paler in colour and possessing a strong white-tipped orange bill. When airborne, greylags converse in ringing tones, 'aakug-ung-ung', and on the ground they gabble like farmyard geese, their domesticated descendants. They nest further south than most other geese with one wild population breeding on moorland in northern Scotland. In addition, breeding stocks have been established by man and there are feral flocks in several parts of Britain. Nesting grounds are vacated in the autumn. Birds move southwards and many migrants arrive from

Iceland, the majority remaining in Scotland, central and eastern parts being most favoured. Like pink-footed geese, they feed on a variety of material obtained from cultivated land. Only a small proportion adopt estuarine sites for roosting.

Left, pink-footed goose; **right,** white-fronted goose; **bottom,** greylag goose

Brent Goose *Branta bernicla* 58-60cm
Barnacle Goose *Branta leucopsis* 58-70cm

These two species of black geese are closely associated with the coast. The brent goose roosts on mudflats and shingle banks and feeds largely on eel grass, *Zostera,* and the green seaweed, *Enteromorpha,* which are uncovered at low tide in estuaries and on shallow shores. In recent years, with a marked increase in numbers, some birds have been feeding on grassland and winter wheat when their usual food supplies were exhausted. This goose breeds in the far north all around the Arctic archipelago, mainly on small islands. In view of its very wide distribution it is not surprising to find there are four races of brent goose, two of which are regular winter visitors to western Europe. In all of them the head, neck and upper breast are black with two white patches on the sides of the neck. The latter markings are absent in juveniles. The back is dark greyish-brown, the feathers having lighter fringes. The dark upper parts contrast with the pure white rump when the birds are seen in flight.

Birds breeding in western Siberia — the dark-bellied race *B.b. bernicla* or Russian brent — winter on the coast of western Europe as far south as Brittany with appreciable numbers crossing the North Sea to take up residence in East Anglia and along the south coast. A light-bellied race, *B.b.hrota*, breeds in Spitsbergen, Greenland and Arctic Canada. This is the Atlantic brent. The Spitsbergen birds migrate to Denmark in winter, a proportion crossing to Lindisfarne on the north-east coast of England, while light-bellied birds from Greenland, and some from Canada, move to Ireland.

The barnacle goose has a black neck and breast setting off a white face and forehead. The upperparts are light grey with darker bars, the belly being distinctly paler.

Barnacle geese are relatively restricted in their distribution. They breed in three places: east Greenland, Spitsbergen and Novaya Zemlya which lies off the north-western coast of Russia. The autumn migration brings all the birds to Britain and a small section of the seaboard of western Europe. Those from Greenland winter in western Scotland and Ireland, particularly on islands such as Islay. The Spitsbergen population moves to the Solway while birds from Russia pass through the Baltic to the flat shores of the Netherlands. They feed on coastal pastures using their stubby bills to crop the short turf and also to dig out the underground shoots of plants like clover which are full of nourishment. Normally they are in large flocks but occasionally one or more birds may become attached to parties of other species.

Below, brent geese; **bottom,** barnacle geese

Shelducks Tribe: Tadornini

Shelducks represent in many ways an intermediate group. As with geese, the sexes are almost alike and the males assist in tending the young. They have longer necks than most ducks but resemble them in having specula and often in their mode of feeding.

Shelduck *Tadorna tadorna* 61cm

The term 'sheld' means variegated or piebald, which aptly describes a shelduck's plumage, a bold mixture of black, white and chestnut. There is a bright red bill, the drake being distinguished by a fleshy knob at the base of the upper mandible.

In Britain the majority of shelducks breed near the coast, being particularly associated with broad, shallow estuaries. They obtain most of their food from soggy mudflats, walking slowly, swinging their bills from side to side, dabbling in the wet surface layers, extracting material from the mud. A favourite food is the tiny snail, *Hydrobia*. Sometimes they swim with their heads submerged sampling the muddy floor.

The shelduck usually nests in tunnel-like holes, in rabbit burrows or under vegetation. These may be in sand dunes or in rough ground adjacent to the coast. After hatching, the young are led to the water and initially are tended by both parents. Family parties are normally seen swimming together towards the end of June, the chicks diving freely when alarmed. Being gregarious, it is not long before several such groups join forces to form a flotilla which can be supervised by a reduced number of adults and this arrangement allows most of the parents to depart in July for moulting.

The moult migration of shelducks in western Europe is a remarkable phenomenon. Birds which have left their young flock together and move to the shallow south-eastern corner of the North Sea where on the Knechtsand, an area rich in mud- and sand-banks, they can rest in safety while shedding and re-forming their flight feathers. Up to 100,000 birds have been counted. A second, and smaller, flock of about 3,000 uses Bridgwater Bay, Somerset. Dispersal from the moulting grounds starts in September when the birds have regained their ability to fly.

Opposite, shelduck (male

30

Dabbling Ducks Tribe: Anatini

These ducks usually feed in shallow water, dabbling in the surface layer for seeds and succulent weeds together with snails and other aquatic animals, and occasionally up-ending and stretching their necks as far as possible to reach food underwater. Some come ashore to forage on land. They are short-legged and when walking hold their bodies more or less horizontal.

Dabbling ducks are probably more often associated with freshwater habitats but two species, apart from the ubiquitous mallard, are often seen in winter in flocks on tidal estuaries.

Wigeon *Anas penelope* 46cm

The wigeon is a summer resident across northern Europe and Asia, a small number breeding in Scotland and northern England. A few pairs nest sporadically elsewhere. At the end of the summer large flocks move southwards, some tarrying in Britain where they feed on muddy coasts, like brent geese, on eel-grass and *Enteromorpha*. They also crop the short grass on saltings together with more lush pastures inland. The drake is identified by his chestnut head which bears a creamy streak bisecting a high crown. In the air, a broad white band along the forewing is distinctive but his call is unique, a high-pitched penetrating whistle, 'whee-oo'.

Pintail *Anas acuta* 61cm

The pintail is one of the most elegant and colourful of the ducks. The chocolate head of the male is slashed on each side by a light streak which joins the white on the front of the neck and breast and belly. At the rear, the dark tail is extended by fine feathery streamers. Pintail breed throughout the northern hemisphere. In Europe the majority nest in central and northern Russia but a few are found in Scotland and also in one or two parts of England, normally not far from the east coast. Winter flocks are attracted to muddy estuarine waters, those of the Dee and the Mersey being particularly favoured. Here they feed by dabbling and up-ending and sometimes they venture inland exploring floodwaters and also stubbles.

Opposite top, wigeon (male); **bottom,** pintail (male)

Diving Ducks Tribe: Aythyini

These are shorter-bodied than dabbling ducks and, having their feet se[t] well back, they shuffle awkwardly on land holding themselves mor[e] upright. They are not fast movers underwater, collecting weed an[d] sedentary animals rather than pursuing fish. When they take off, they ar[e] obliged to patter over the water before becoming airborne.

One species in this group can be described as marine since it spends mos[t] of its life at sea. Others appear occasionally on estuaries.

Scaup *Aythya marila* 48cm

This is a winter visitor normally seen on shallow offshore waters o[r] broad estuaries. It occurs in very large flocks, the largest numbers i[n] Britain being recorded in the Firth of Forth although these do no[t] match those in the southern Baltic and the Wadden Zee adjacent t[o] the Dutch coast. It dives for hard-shelled molluscs, particularl[y] mussels, but will also take vegetable material, spent grain fro[m] Scottish distilleries frequently proving attractive. In summer it i[s] found on lakes set in the tundra of northern Europe, Asia an[d] America, building its nest on the ground not far from the water. Whil[e] there are some records of nesting in Britain, it is not a regular breeder

The scaup drake has a black head, neck and breast and the tail is als[o] dark while the feathers on the back are light grey and vermiculated[.] Thus at a distance birds floating on the water appear as two dar[k] extremities separated by a lighter zone. The female is greyish-brow[n] and her flanks lack the brightness of her mate's. Her specia[l] distinguishing feature is a broad band of white around the base of th[e] bill.

Tufted Duck *Aythya fuligula* 43cm

This duck is normally found on inland waters but sometimes in winte[r] small parties appear on estuaries and they may associate with scaup[.] The male is distinctly black and white although the dark head ofte[n] has a purple sheen. There is no greyness, thus preventing confusio[n] with scaup, and his mate does not sport the broad blaze of whit[e] around the bill. Both species have bright yellow eyes and pale blu[e] bills, that of the scaup being more robust.

Opposite top, scaup (male); **bottom,** tufted duck (male[)]

35

Eider ducks

Sea Ducks Tribe: Mergini

This tribe includes a number of species, all of which are carnivorous, diving for molluscs and crustaceans or actively pursuing fish. In winter most of them are found in shallow coastal waters but many breed inland close to fresh water.

Eider *Somateria mollissima* 58cm

This is the most numerous of European sea ducks and in Britain breeds as far south as Northumberland on the eastern seaboard and Walney Island in the west. Colonies are also established in Northern Ireland. Non-breeding birds may be seen offshore around the British and Irish coastlines throughout the year and these are joined by small numbers of mature adults in winter.

In spring, when pairs are together, there is a marked difference between the sexes, the male appearing largely black and white while his mate, like many ducks, is fawnish-brown with darker bars. Both birds are short necked and heavily built, the heaviness being especially apparent in the head which is wedge-shaped. On closer examination the drake is seen to be not completely pied, the sides of the head and the nape being pale green in colour while the breast is often tinged with pink.

Eiders feed largely on marine animals such as mussels and crabs, many being obtained by diving. In the shallowest waters food may be reached by dipping the head below the surface or by up-ending. The sturdy bill allows the eider to deal effectively with hard-shelled prey.

Nests are built on the ground, often in the open, of grasses and occasionally seaweed. They are lined with down, eider-down, from the duck's breast. The drake plays no part after the clutch has been laid and by July he is moulting. Afterwards he is almost completely black except for one area of whiteness on the wing, remaining in this state until the end of the year when a second moult re-establishes the full breeding dress.

Eider duck incubating

Long-tailed duck:
left, male (winter);
right, female (winter)

Long-tailed Duck *Clangula hyemalis* Male 55cm. Female 41cm
This species breeds in the high Arctic, further north than any other
duck. It is wholly marine in winter and is present in shallow waters,
diving for food which includes mussels, winkles and crabs. Large
flocks are seen in the Baltic and parties may be present around the
mainland of Scotland and the Isles while, further south, groups may
put in an appearance at places such as the Wash on the east coast of
England.

The long-tailed duck differs from other ducks in having three
moults each year, winter plumage differing from breeding dress. In
winter the distinctly round head and the neck of the drake are white
with chocolate-brown patches below and behind the eye, around
which is a thickened ring. The breast is brown and there is a dark
strand along the mid-line of the back joining the similarly-coloured
streamers of the tail. This plumage lasts from October until March,
the period during which long-tailed ducks are most likely to be seen
around the coast. At this time the female is mainly greyish-brown
except for a white head with dusky smudges beneath the eyes and a
crown bisected by a brown band. Moulting starts in April, summer
plumage being distinctly darker.

Common Scoter *Melanitta nigra* 48cm
Numbers of common scoters visit Britain in winter, large flocks being
seen offshore. They are heavily-built birds which float buoyantly on
the water, the drakes being entirely black except for a strip of orange-
yellow running over the upper surface of the bill from the large knob
at the base. The females are dark brown but the sides of the head and

Common scoter: **left,** male; **right,** female

throat are distinctly paler. They take off with some difficulty and fly close to the surface in lines or in wedge-shaped formations. As with other sea ducks they dive freely and the major part of their food consists of hard-shelled molluscs such as mussels.

Apart from some immature birds, common scoters leave coastal waters in spring. They move northwards, most of those which have wintered in Britain probably breeding in northern Europe close to freshwater lakes set in coniferous forests or treeless tundra. A small number nest in Scotland, moorland dotted with small lochs being the typical habitat. Northern Ireland also has a small population.

Velvet Scoter *Melanitta fusca* 56cm
Velvet scoters are winter visitors to British waters and are usually seen in small parties which are often associated with flocks of the more numerous common scoter. Apart from size they are distinguished by the whiteness of the secondaries on the wings, a feature which is very evident in an airborne bird but not always when it is floating on the water. Additionally, the male has a white spot beneath the eye and each side of the bill is yellow while the female's head is marked with

Velvet scoter: **left,** male; **right,** female

pale areas both in front of and behind the eyes.

Velvet scoters do not nest in Britain. Birds wintering in European waters have probably bred in Scandinavia and western Siberia. They moult in the Baltic, some then moving further afield. There are other populations in eastern Siberia and also in North America where this species is known as the white-winged scoter.

Goldeneye *Bucephala clangula* 45cm

Appreciable numbers of this species winter on the coastal and estuarine waters of Britain with small groups appearing inland on large lakes and reservoirs. As with other sea ducks it dives for food, usually in places which are relatively shallow.

Apart from the golden eye, at a distance the male looks black and white but, at closer quarters, the large and very characteristic triangular head shows a green gloss with a round white patch between the eye and the bill. Another distinctive feature is the striping on the flanks where the white underparts meet the darker wings. The female is similar in shape to the male, a brown head being separated from a greyish body by a white collar.

Goldeneye: **left,** male; **right,** female

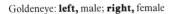

The goldeneye breeds in the sub-Arctic coniferous forest zone of Europe, Asia and America, normally laying its eggs in holes in trees. Since 1970 a few pairs have nested in Scotland, the provision of nest boxes having been beneficial.

Smew *Mergus albellus* 40cm

This is the smallest of the ducks known as sawbills, which have the edges of their narrow bills armed with 'teeth' to facilitate the grasping of fish taken, along with molluscs and crustaceans, during diving

Smew: **left,** male; **right,** female

forays. As with the goldeneye, it is a summer resident in the coniferous forests of northern Europe and Asia, laying its eggs in tree-holes. It winters further south, the Ijsselmeer in the Netherlands being the most popular area in Europe but single birds or small parties may be seen in Britain, more particularly in the south-east. They tend to appear in very hard weather on sheltered coastal sites and also inland where there is open water.

In winter dress the male is mainly white with some darker markings, a black patch surrounding the eye and dark streaks curving from the crown into the nape of the neck. A black strand runs along the back and, since the wing tips are also dark, a flying bird looks distinctly pied. Female smew are chestnut-capped with white cheeks and necks, the general body colour being greyish.

Red-breasted Merganser *Mergus serrator* 58cm

This is a typical sawbill which breeds across Europe, Asia and North America. In Britain it is common in Scotland with smaller numbers in north-west England and in Wales, nesting on the ground close to both fresh and salt water. Mainly marine in winter, birds can sometimes be

Red-breasted merganser:
left, male; **right,** female

seen fishing in shallow water, swimming with necks outstretched looking for prey before diving.

The drake's elongated red bill protrudes from a dark green head which bears a horizontal wispy crest. There is a broad white collar above a streaky brown breast and while the upper parts are dark, rows of small white windows are apparent on the shoulders and more continuous strands on the folded wings. The female's head is similarly crested and, apart from a dull white throat, the overall colour is chestnut and this merges into the greyer tones of the back and chest. The drake starts to moult as early as May and in eclipse plumage is very much like his mate until his breeding dress is acquired toward the end of the year.

Goosander *Mergus merganser* 66cm

Like the merganser this species breeds in both the Old and the New Worlds, favouring wooded country with freshwater lakes and rivers, laying its eggs in hollow trees or in hidden cavities at ground level. Goosanders started to breed in Scotland in 1871. They have prospered, now being well established in the Borders and in northern England. In winter they still show a preference for freshwater but move to estuaries and sheltered bays when lakes and rivers are frozen.

Floating high in the water, the drake, at a distance, looks dark above and white below. On closer inspection the head is seen to be bottle green but it lacks the wispy crest of the merganser and the breast is white rather than brown. The female resembles a merganser in having a chestnut head but she can be distinguished by a white chin which is sharply defined, as is the junction between the neck and the breast. Like the merganser, the drake moults early and in eclipse is very much like his mate.

Goosander: **left,** male; **right,** female

WADERS

Birds referred to as waders are usually long-legged, frequently long-necked and often long-billed. They are adapted for feeding in wet terrain such as freshly-exposed coastal mud and sand flats together with the margins of shallow inland waters and soggy marshland. They are included within four families:

Oystercatchers (Haematopodidae), Avocets and Stilts (Recurvirostridae), Plovers (Charadriidae), Sandpipers, Shanks and Phalaropes (Scolopacidae).

OYSTERCATCHERS Family: Haematopodidae

Oystercatchers are strongly built birds with pied or black plumage and brightly coloured legs, bills and eyes. The forward pointing toes are slightly webbed and the birds are normally encountered at the coast where they use their powerful, laterally compressed bills to secure food. Their nests are saucer-like scrapes among outcropping rocks, on shingle, sand or on turf. Chicks, in down, leave the nest as soon as they are dry.

Oystercatcher *Haematopus ostralegus* 43cm

The oystercatcher breeds all round the British coast wherever it is free from disturbance. During the present century some birds have moved inland, breeding on the gravelly margins of rivers and lakes, on arable

Oystercatcher

land and even on moors. Inland nesting is common in Scotland and northern England with local examples further south as in East Anglia where it occurs on damp pastures not too far removed from the sea or waterways.

On sandy or muddy shores oystercatchers feed on bivalve molluscs such as cockles. They pull them to the surface and separate the two halves either by driving their bill between them and then prising them apart, or by first hammering a hole in the hard casing and subsequently severing the thick muscle which holds the two half-shells together. The succulent contents are then extracted. On rocky shores limpets are chipped from their anchorages, the oystercatcher using its bill as a pickaxe.

Chicks are fed by their parents until they become effective feeders. Juvenile birds are not as dark as the adults and have white collars across their throats as do oystercatchers of all ages in winter. At this time there are large flocks in shallow estuaries made up of some local birds together with migrants from further north.

AVOCETS Family: Recurvirostridae

Avocets are large pied birds with long legs. They are elegant waders, their bills being slender, elongated and upturned. Some webbing connects the three forward-pointing toes and these birds swim readily. Breeding occurs in colonies, the nests being scrapes on the ground, usually very close to the water.

Avocet *Recurvirostra avosetta* 43cm

The avocet requires a habitat with shallow lagoons of brackish water where it can wade and feed together with open flats for nesting. In north-western Europe such areas are found on the low-lying coasts of southern Sweden, Denmark, Holland and Germany. Regrettably the species disappeared from Britain in the first half of the nineteenth century but, since 1947 and 1963 respectively, two carefully-managed sites at Minsmere and Havergate Island in Suffolk have attracted colonies and, more recently, birds have nested elsewhere along the East Anglian coast. Being migratory avocets are also seen on passage, many of them probably wintering in the shallow salt lakes of East Africa although a few may linger in estuarine locations in Devon and Cornwall.

Avocet

The avocet supports its black and white body on thin blue-grey legs which are of such a length as to project well beyond the tail in flight. When wading in the shallows the uniquely-shaped bill held partly open is swung from side to side filtering off small aquatic animals from the water. In deeper conditions where the bird must swim it sometimes up-ends like a duck to sample the muddy bottom.

PLOVERS Family: Charadriidae

Plovers are small to medium sized, compactly built and often have colourful patterned plumage. In contrast to other waders their bills are relatively short and are unsuitable for probing in wet sand or mud. As a result they are mainly surface feeders and move in energetic short bursts, pausing every now and then with head erect to see if there are any small creatures visible which may be taken by surprise. In addition they often use 'pattering' to attract prey, one foot being pattered rapidly on the ground, such movements often encouraging worms and other creatures to move to the surface. They do not wade in the true sense, usually feeding along the water's edge or on open stretches of wetland.

Ringed plover

Ringed Plover *Charadrius hiaticula* 19cm

This species is the most familiar plover found on British shores. It is called the ringed plover because of the black and white collar encircling the neck. There is, in addition, a black eyestripe which joins dark bands passing above the bill and across the white forehead. Thus the head has a pied appearance although the rest of the plumage is sandy coloured above and white below. The bill is orange-yellow tipped with black and the legs are yellowish. Ringed plovers are stocky little birds running here and there over the shore, bobbing nervously when disturbed and sometimes taking brief flights during which a white bar is apparent on the wing. In the air and on the ground the call is a sad liquid note 'too-ee'.

On low-lying coasts nests are found on sand or shingle. When the risk of disturbance is high the birds show some flexibility, sometimes hiding their nests beneath shoreline plants such as shrubby seablite or moving to adjacent farmland. In addition, some breed on the stony margins of rivers and lakes while others take to gravel pits and similar habitats.

Ringed plovers are present throughout the year, although many British birds winter across the Channel and as far south as Africa, being replaced by visitors from farther north.

Golden plover (northern race)

Golden Plover *Pluvialis apricaria* 28cm

Outside the breeding season golden plovers are in flocks which in coastal areas avoid the shores but which are seen on the saltings and other open ground near the sea. They feed for the most part on small invertebrates picked up from the surface of the ground.

In winter the underparts of the golden plover are white while the dark feathers of the back and wings are edged with a distinctive shade of gold. The light flanks and breast have scattered dusky markings. By spring the birds have developed their breeding dress and black feathers now clothe both the belly and a variable amount of the breast. Members of the northern race which breeds on the Arctic tundra in Iceland, northern Scandinavia and Russia have blackness extending from the face to the belly while British birds, which are members of the southern race, may have little black on the breast. The latter breed on upland moors.

Birds nesting in the far north move southwards after the end of the breeding season but many British birds take up residence in lowland areas not too far removed from the breeding grounds. Others may reach as far south as the Mediterranean. Early in the year companies of birds begin to migrate northwards and as they pass overhead it is possible to hear their musical flight call 'too-ee'.

Grey plover in winter plumage

Grey Plover *Pluvialis squatarola* 28cm

In contrast to the golden plover this species is a shorebird and i
occurs, singly or in small parties, in the company of other waders such
as dunlins, amongst which it is seen to be a much larger bird. It is als
less active and has a characteristic hunched stance.

In winter dress the upper parts are covered with dark feather
fringed with white but the rump is pure white, as is the belly. A
distinctive feature at all seasons is the black 'armpit' evident when the
bird flies. With the approach of spring black feathers now cover the
underparts from the face to the belly, the pattern being similar to tha
seen in the northern form of the golden plover, but the darkly speckled
upper parts show no trace of gold.

Grey plovers breed in Arctic Russia and America well beyond the
tree limit on the tundra. They winter further south and while some
halt in Britain the majority are passage migrants probably reaching
South African shores.

Lapwing

Lapwing *Vanellus vanellus* 30cm

Lapwings may breed on coastal marshes and at this time the cocks indulge in energetic display flights, tumbling and twisting in the air on blunt tipped wings, screaming excitedly. Once breeding is finished, flocks are formed which stay together throughout the winter. They may be seen on pastures and arable land and also on coastal and estuarine mud flats, especially in hard weather. They feed like typical plovers, running a short distance, halting and then pouncing on any victim which may be visible.

Seen at a distance lapwings appear almost black and white but closer inspection reveals many subtle shades of metallic green and the under-tail coverts are rufous. In the autumn the crest is much reduced and the feathers on the back are duller with light golden-brown edgings. The blackness on the chin and throat is lost and this winter plumage is very similar to that of juvenile birds where the lighter fringes on the feathers of the upper parts creates a distinctly scaly effect. By early spring breeding dress is re-established.

Some flocks of birds from western Europe may winter in Britain, arriving as early as July. After moulting they may, along with British birds, move further to the south or west.

SANDPIPERS, SHANKS AND PHALAROPES Family Scolopacidae

This large family of true wading birds includes examples ranging from small to large, with their bills and legs showing considerable variation in shape and size. Many of them feed while wading in shallow water or moving over wet sand or mud, the length of the bill determining the depth to which they can reach. Their plumage generally lacks the strong patterns of the plovers, the upper parts being mottled in various shades of grey or brown with lighter underparts which may be modified when a bird is in breeding dress by the addition of other shades to the breast and belly.

Knot *Calidris canutus* 25cm

Knots breed in the high Arctic on damp lichen-covered tundra. This is inhospitable terrain and the birds are only in residence for about two months of the year. After nesting they disperse to the south, birds from different areas having different wintering grounds. Those from north-eastern Canada and Greenland come to western Europe, others travelling as far as South Africa, South America and Australia.

In Britain knots occur most often in the inter-tidal zone of wide estuaries where there are great expanses of sand and mud. They form dense flocks, frequently numbered in thousands, which resemble

Knot (juvenile)

billowing smoke-like clouds in the air. When airborne, the birds emit a soft call note, 'knut', which gives the name to the species. They feed together in crowded masses, inserting their slender bills into the surface layers, extracting prey such as Macoma and *Hydrobia*.

In winter plumage, shades of grey predominate but in spring there is a marked change, the back now being covered with black feathers edged with rufous while the neck, breast and belly are chestnut-red.

Sanderling *Calidris alba* 20cm
This is another species breeding in the high Arctic. Most of the birds seen in Britain are passage migrants moving southwards from Greenland and Siberia. A few remain throughout the winter. They are generally in small parties, moving at speed along the tide-line looking for sandhoppers and shrimps left by each retreating wavelet. This habit makes them almost unmistakable. Those birds which pass through may reach South Africa.

In winter plumage, sanderlings are light in colour. The underparts and the facial area are pure white, the upper parts are pale grey except for a dark mark on the 'wrist' of the closed wing. They change in spring — the head, breast and upper parts becoming a rich chestnut which is darkly speckled, the belly remaining white. Sanderlings are among the tamest of birds; on the shore they seem reluctant to fly but when they do a prominent white wing-bar is very evident.

Sanderling in winter plumage

Little Stint *Calidris minuta* 14cm

This species is the smallest of the waders seen at the coast. Although it can be present in large flocks it is more often seen in very small groups in the company of other waders such as dunlins. Its breeding range is relatively compact starting in north-eastern Norway and extending across Arctic Europe to western Siberia. Most birds winter in Central and South Africa and little stints are therefore seen in Britain on passage, mainly in the autumn. A few linger in southern Britain throughout the winter.

The majority of the birds seen in the autumn are juveniles which were hatched earlier in the year. The feathers covering the upper parts are dark and fringed with rufous. Creamy lines are evident along the edges of the mantle. They run backwards from the shoulders, the two meeting to form a 'V'. The underparts are white with the sides of the breast showing a trace of buff with some darker streaks. Adults in winter dress are more grey-brown but in spring the colouring is much richer, more rufous, this tone being present on the face, neck and breast. At all seasons the legs are very dark as is the short bill.

Temminck's Stint *Calidris temminckii* 15cm

Not as numerous as the little stint, this species is seen in tidal creeks and shallow marsh pools rather than on the open shore. It is a greyer bird than the little stint, with some feathers on the back having dark centres, while the legs are much lighter in colour. When disturbed it towers upwards before moving off.

Birds seen at the coast are migrating, moving from their tundra breeding grounds in Scandinavia and Russia to their winter quarters in tropical Africa. A few pairs have nested in Scotland in recent times.

Left, little stint (juvenile); **right,** Temminck's stint

Curlew sandpiper (juvenile)

Curlew Sandpiper *Calidris ferruginea* 19cm

The curlew sandpiper breeds far away in Arctic Asia and winters in southern latitudes, many birds being present in central and southern Africa. In Britain it is a passage migrant, seen more frequently in the autumn than in the spring.

In breeding dress the curlew sandpiper is unmistakable. The head, chest and underparts are a warm chestnut-red. The bird holds itself upright on longish black legs and the fine-tipped black bill is slightly decurved. When airborne it is distinguished by the unmarked white rump. In winter the upper parts are grey and the breast and belly largely white. Those adults passing through Britain in the autumn will be moulting and losing their bright summer garb but the majority of the birds seen at this time will be juveniles with light underparts tinted with buff on the sides of the breast; this warm colour also fringing the dark feathers clothing the upper parts.

Purple sandpiper (non-breeding)

Purple Sandpiper *Calidris maritima* 20cm
This portly bird with short dull-yellow legs is present throughout the winter on ice-free shores. Occurring singly or in small parties, purple sandpipers prefer rocky coasts and rarely stray very far from spray-splashed rocks. Stone-built jetties and groynes are often occupied. At this season the head, breast and upper parts are dark smoky-grey with dusky streaks on the paler flanks. The edges of the wing coverts are fringed with a lighter tone. The longish dark bill is yellow at the base.

In spring the overall colour is much lighter with the feathers covering the upper parts being edged with chestnut and white and, at this time, the birds move northwards to breed at a number of separate Arctic locations around the Polar basin. When they return in the late autumn the adults are in winter dress while juveniles have chestnut fringes to the dark feathers of the mantle.

Dunlin in summer plumage

Dunlin *Calidris alpina* 17-19cm

This is the most numerous of the small waders seen around the coast in winter. It may be in small parties or in flocks which can be numbered in thousands. This is a compactly built bird with a fairly long black bill which is used almost continuously, exploring wet mud for food. In breeding dress, as with several other waders, the feathers of the upper parts are fringed with chestnut but the most characteristic feature is the black area on the white belly.

There are several races. Those birds wintering around Britain will have bred in northern Scandinavia and north-west Russia. Some dunlins nest in Britain on coastal marshes and moorland and these spend the winter as far away as Africa. When birds are moving southwards in the late summer and autumn they may still be in summer plumage but this is soon lost, the upper parts becoming a dull grey-brown and the dark area below being replaced by uniformly white feathers.

Black-tailed Godwit *Limosa limosa* 41cm

The black-tailed godwit has a rather upright stance, the impression being enhanced by the way it lifts its feet almost vertically when it walks while holding its slim neck erect. Its long slender bill may be very slightly upturned. The general coloration is greyish-brown in winter but in breeding dress the head, neck and breast are a light chestnut with dark bars on the lower breast and belly. Darker feathers clothe the back. When flying, each wing is seen to have a conspicuous white bar and the tail shows a broad terminal band of black below a white rump. In addition, the underwing is also white so that in the air the bird looks distinctly pied and the long legs project beyond the tail.

This species breeds in wet tussocky grasslands. It occurred as a summer resident in England until about 1830, East Anglian grazing marshes being particularly favoured. After being absent for more than a hundred years it has, since 1952, been re-established on the Ouse Washes which offer a good area of undisturbed rough wetland. A few birds have nested sporadically elsewhere. Abroad, the breeding range extends from southern Sweden, Denmark and Holland across Europe and Asia with a small population in Iceland.

Bar-tailed Godwit *Limosa lapponica* 38cm

This species breeds in the Arctic tundra of Europe and Asia. Moving southwards in the late summer, some birds winter in Britain but the majority go much further, many of them reaching Africa.

In breeding dress, the head, neck and underparts of the male are chestnut-red while the dark-centred feathers of the back are fringed with chestnut. There are no dark bars on the belly. His mate is less brightly coloured with only a suggestion of warmth on the neck and breast. Neither bird has the striking white wing-bar seen in the black-tailed godwit. In winter, both birds are grey-brown above with dusky breasts, the rest of the underparts being white. In the air, a white 'V' extends from the rump up the back as in the curlew and whimbrel. At all seasons the tail is barred.

Bar-tailed godwits are usually seen on flatter shores, especially broad estuaries, near the tide-line, thrusting their long bills into the wet sand and mud in their endless search for food.

Opposite top, black-tailed godwit; **bottom,** bar-tailed godwit

Summer

Winter

Summer

Winter

57

Curlew

Curlew *Numenius arquata* 60cm

The curlew is Britain's largest wader and its long downward curving bill allows easy recognition, both on the ground and in the air. It is almost 15cm long in the female, rather less in the male, allowing the bird to probe and reach deeper-burrowing shellfish and marine worms. Although some immature birds may be seen around the coast in early summer the adults do not appear before July or August. Many will have bred on moorland or rough grassland in Britain or northern Europe and some will remain through the winter while others progress southwards towards Africa. In winter, parties of curlews are commonplace, individuals being loosely scattered over the flats, each one silhouetted against the glistening mud. They are renowned for their shyness and, if disturbed, take off often calling 'coor-li' as they go. In flight they are greyish-brown above except for a wedge of white extending from the rump to the lower back. The underparts are darkly speckled. There is no marked difference between summer and winter plumages, winter dress being rather colder in tone.

Whimbrel

Whimbrel *Numenius phaeopus* 45cm

The whimbrel is curlew-like in form, but smaller. It is slightly darker in colour with a special distinguishing feature, a distinctively patterned crown with two dark bands flanking a lighter coloured median streak. It breeds rather more to the north than the curlew although the ranges of the two species show some overlapping. In Britain the Shetlands are its stronghold with a few birds in the Hebrides and some sporadic breeding elsewhere. Consequently in most of Britain whimbrels are regarded as passage migrants. The most typical sightings are in May when small groups pass overhead flying northwards. They converse in the air, the note being a tittering 'titti-titti-titti-tit' and sometimes described as the seven whistles. On occasion birds halt briefly to rest and feed. If they do so in the company of curlews, the difference in size is apparent and also the fact that they are much more approachable. In the autumn the return journey takes them to the warmer shores of southern Europe and Africa.

Redshank *Tringa totanus* 28cm

Redshanks are present around the coast throughout the year. They are commonest on the muddy flats of broad tidal estuaries where they are versatile feeders, taking crustaceans such as *Corophium* from the superficial layers and probing for ragworms which are more deeply entrenched. At high water they may roost communally.

The redshank is distinguished by the long orange-red legs and the well-developed bill, approximately 5cm long, which is also orange coloured at the base. In summer the upper parts are greyish-brown, although they lose some of their warmth in winter, while the lighter underparts are darkly streaked. Few birds are more excitable and demonstrative. At the approach of an intruder it takes off issuing a rapid-fire 'tu-tu-tu' which becomes a more staccato 'teuk-teuk-teuk' when real danger threatens. In the air, the flight is rather erratic, the bird tilting from side to side as it goes, showing a white rump together with a blunt triangular white bar along the rear edge of each wing. On alighting it holds its wings erectly over the body in wader fashion but for longer than most.

Some redshanks nest close to the shore among the marram grass of sand dunes or on coastal saltings. Others move inland to damp grasslands. Those which have been winter visitors fly north to Iceland and Scandinavia but they do not populate the Arctic shores of Russia, preferring more temperate conditions. After breeding, the general urge to migrate shown by many species is not apparent in the redshank. While some populations may move to more southern shores for the winter others may be almost sedentary.

A second red-legged wader, the spotted redshank, *Tringa erythropus*, 30cm, is a passage migrant seen as it moves between its breeding grounds in northern Europe and Asia and its winter quarters around the Mediterranean and in Central Africa. In breeding dress it is sooty-black in colour, the upper parts being spotted with white. By autumn it is much lighter, pearly grey above with white underparts. It is a much leggier bird than the common redshank, the very slender bill is longer and the relatively small head is carried on a slim neck. In the air it can be differentiated by the absence of whiteness on the trailing edge of the wing and also by its flight call, a bisyllabic 'chew-it'.

Opposite, redshank

60

Greenshank (juvenile)

Greenshank *Tringa nebularia* 30cm

A greenshank is marginally larger than a redshank and can b
differentiated at close quarters by the colour of its legs, pale green, an
the blue-grey bill which is very slightly upcurved. The upper parts ar
greyer than those of a redshank and very pale in winter at which tim
the underparts are almost completely white. In breeding dress th
head, neck, upper breast and flanks are streaked and spotted dar
brown, these markings largely disappearing in the autumn. In the ai
the dark wings are unmarked but the whiteness apparent on the bac
and rump extends into the tail. Although like a redshank it calls 'tu-tu
tu', the pitch of the notes is lower.

The greenshank's breeding range extends from the Scottis
Highlands across Eurasia, nesting occurring on moorland, tundra an
in forest clearings. Many of the birds which frequent the western par
of the range may winter as far south as Africa but a small number ma
tarry in southern Britain on sheltered shores. In coastal area
greenshanks are most evident in the autumn when birds are o
passage, many of them being juveniles which are rather browner tha
their parents.

Common Sandpiper *Actitis hypoleucos* 20cm

The common sandpiper is not difficult to recognise. It moves with a characteristic bobbing motion picking up morsels of food as it goes. Any brief pause is marked by wagtail-like movements of the tail end of the body. If it is disturbed it takes off for a short flight, bursts of flickering wing-beats alternating with brief glides during which the wings are held rigid at the end of a downstroke. The alarm note is a shrill 'twee-wee-wee'. When airborne a well-defined wing bar is apparent but the rump and the tail, apart from the lighter edges, are the same colour as the greenish-brown upper parts. While the underparts are largely white, a special feature is the dark colouring on the sides of the breast which forms the anterior border of a white strip extending upwards from the lower part of the breast in front of the carpal joint of the closed wing. Juveniles are similar to their parents with some feathers of the upper parts showing buff fringes.

In Britain the common sandpiper nests not far from water by upland streams and tarns but also on sheltered, undisturbed coasts. It breeds in most countries of northern Europe and Asia. At other times of the year the occasional bird may be seen not far from the breeding range but the majority migrate, covering considerable distances before reaching their winter quarters in the tropics or beyond. They can be seen on passage, single birds or small groups feeding in quiet creeks and drains.

Two other sandpipers, the wood sandpiper, *Tringa glareola*, 20cm, and the green sandpiper, *Tringa ochropus*, 23cm, are passage migrants through Britain, more often seen in tidal creeks than on the open shore.

A wood sandpiper is longer-legged and slimmer than a common sandpiper, and the upper parts are boldly speckled; those of the juvenile being bright buff. There is no white wing bar but the rump is light in colour, features which are apparent when the bird is airborne as is the whiteness of the shaft of the outermost flight feather. The alarm note, 'chiff-chiff-chiff', issued when a bird is flushed, is very distinctive.

The green sandpiper is very dark above, the darkness extending to the lower surface of the wings. In such a setting the white rump is especially prominent and at all times the bird is boldly marked, appearing almost black and white. The only parts which approximate

Common sandpiper (juvenile)

to green are the legs. It is a shy bird and tends to rest and feed where there is good cover. When taken by surprise it calls shrilly 'weet-a-weet' as it towers upwards before flying off.

Both species breed across northern Europe and Asia. The wood sandpiper usually nests on the ground in bogs, marshes and thinly wooded areas while the green sandpiper normally takes over the discarded nests of tree-nesting species such as thrushes. Both birds are active migrants, wood sandpipers wintering for the most part in southern parts of the Old World, most green sandpipers tending to stay north of the equator.

Left, turnstone brooding; **right,** turnstone in summer plumage

Turnstone *Arenaria interpres* 23cm

The turnstone is renowned for its specialist mode of feeding. It moves methodically about the shore flicking aside with its bill shells, stones and litter to uncover any small animals which may be hidden underneath. Rocky and stony coastlines suit it best.

When in breeding dress a turnstone has its upper parts richly mottled in chestnut and black and, while underneath it is light in colour, the breast is black with dark bands running to the eye, neck and shoulder. As a result the bird looks black and white from a distance and also when in flight. It has orange legs, but being only half the size of an oystercatcher, and with a much shorter and duller bill, there is no confusion.

Turnstones nest on the lichen-covered tundra adjacent to the Arctic shores of Europe, Asia and America. In the autumn they move southwards to their winter quarters which may be beyond the equator. A few non-breeding birds may be seen in Britain throughout the summer and some are present in winter, at which time their plumage is not richly coloured, the upper parts being dusky-brown.

Left, red-necked phalarope (winter); **right,** grey phalarope (winter)

Red-necked Phalarope *Phalaropus lobatus* 16.5cm
Grey Phalarope *Phalaropus fulicarius* 20cm

Phalaropes are small sandpiper-like birds which, as passage migrants, are usually seen swimming, not wading, in small coastal pools and shallow tidal waters. They float buoyantly with their long necks erect and swim erratically with bobbing heads darting this way and that, snapping up insects and other aquatic creatures. Occasionally they spin round on the surface so as to create a vortex sucking up material from below. Swimming is facilitated by the presence of lobes on the toes which make them more effective paddles.

Both species spend the winter at sea in warmer parts of the three oceans. The grey phalarope breeds on the Arctic tundra adjacent to the coastline of both the Old and New Worlds, Iceland being a southern outpost. The red-necked phalarope does not penetrate as far north, its range including northern Norway and Iceland with some birds nesting in Shetland and, less securely, in northern Scotland, the Hebrides and Orkney. Many of these birds winter in the Arabian Sea.

Phalaropes are seen more frequently in Britain on autumn passage than in spring. They are usually in winter plumage, grey-and-white birds with each eye set in a strip of black. Although the two are similar, the larger grey phalarope is lighter and more uniformly grey, its bill is shorter and broader than the dark needle-like one of the smaller species. Spring sees a complete transformation. The grey phalarope acquires a reddish neck and underparts and the head is black-capped with white cheeks. The red-necked remains light underneath but develops an orange-red band on the side of the neck while the head and upper parts are slate-grey with some rufous streaks.

Great skua

SKUAS Family: Stercorariidae

Skuas are dark coloured seabirds which obtain an appreciable part of their food by harrying other species, usually gulls and terns in flight, and obliging them to disgorge. They are powerful fliers with long pointed and angled wings and are capable of out-manoeuvering most other birds in the air. In addition to chasing in hawk-like fashion they possess hooked bills and claws. A special feature is the shape of the tail which is wedge-shaped with the central feathers projecting. Although dark brown in colour there is a flash of white on the outstretched wing and the plumage, except for the great skua, can vary with light and dark phase birds. Two species are summer residents in Britain.

Great Skua *Stercocarius skua* 58cm

The great skua or bonxie is slightly larger than a herring gull but is uniformly brown except for the white patch at the base of the primaries on both surfaces of the wing. In summer when it is in residence, apart from pursuing other birds to make them discard food,

67

it is a considerable predator, taking small mammals and the eggs, young and adults of species such as puffins and waders.

Races of the great skua breed along the edge of the Antarctic continent, skuas having been recorded further south than any other bird. They are regular tenants of penguin-breeding colonies. In the northern hemisphere nesting is mainly confined to Iceland, the Faeroes, the Shetlands and the Orkneys with a few pairs in the extreme of Scotland. They favour rough grassy moorland close to the sea where small, loosely-knit communities are established and jealously guarded against intruders.

At the end of the nesting season they move southwards, more particularly along the east coast towards the Channel, before dispersing to their winter quarters in the north Atlantic where they are sometimes observed following ships, scavenging for offal and other waste.

Arctic Skua *Stercocarius parasiticus* 46cm

The Arctic skua is distinctly smaller than the great skua. In addition the elongated tail feathers are much more pronounced and this is a species in which there are two distinct colour phases. Dark phase birds are almost uniformly brown whereas light phase individuals have light underparts, some birds showing coloration of an intermediate nature.

When breeding, Arctic skuas are restricted to the northern hemisphere and colonies are found all round the Polar basin. In Britain they are confined to the northernmost parts of Scotland and the Northern and Western Isles where they are found in small groups on moorland. The nest is a simple scrape and often, near by, is a small hillock or tufted elevation acting as a 'lookout' post for the sitting bird's mate. They do not arrive on their breeding grounds before May.

Apart from harassing other birds, forcing them to yield any food which is being carried, they also take the occasional small bird or mammal, insects and, in the autumn, moorland fruits such as crowberries.

In the late summer and autumn Arctic skuas are seen moving down the coast. They are considerable travellers, many wintering in the southern hemisphere.

Opposite top, Arctic skua (dark phase); **bottom,** light phase

GULLS Family: Laridae

This is a large family of long-winged seabirds, many being heavily built and possessing stout and slightly hooked bills appropriate to their roles as scavengers and predators. Their tails are squared or rounded and the adults of most species have white underparts with grey or black backs. Some are white-headed whereas others have dark coloured hoods which are much reduced in winter, at which time the white-headed species acquire some dusky feathers. Their sturdy legs, with webbed feet, are often brightly coloured, as are their bills.

Most gulls are gregarious and nest in colonies. After hatching the chicks remain at or near the nest site, being fed by the parents on regurgitated food. Juveniles are unlike their parents, often being darkly mottled and with a black band towards the end of the tail. The gradual development of adult plumage may take two to four years. Six species of gull nest regularly in Britain.

Black-headed Gull *Larus ridibundus* 38cm

This is the smallest common resident gull. In breeding dress the head

Black-headed gull in summer plumage

Black-headed gull in winter plumage

s chocolate-brown except for a white ring around the eye and both the
bill and the legs are red. In flight, a white leading edge to the wing is
noticeable. By autumn, apart from a dark mark behind the eye, the
head is white.

Gulleries are established at the coast on low-lying sites such as sand
dunes and shingle ridges. They are often associated with groups of
other species, especially terns. Many birds nest inland on moors, by
reed-fringed meres and also at man-made sites such as flooded gravel
pits. Juvenile birds have mottled grey-brown upper parts, darker
feathers on the back of the lighter head and the bill is yellow, tipped
with black. The white tail terminates in a black band. When one year
old, some brownish feathers are still apparent on the wings and the bill
and legs are distinctly duller than in the adult.

In winter, when numbers of immigrants arrive in Britain from
further north, this is the gull best known to town-dwellers. While
some birds remain around the coast others move inland frequenting
rubbish dumps and often descending on gardens to pick up household
scraps. In the countryside considerable flocks follow the plough,
competing noisily for freshly-uncovered worms and grubs. Such birds
often roost communally on open waters such as reservoirs.

Common gull

Common Gull *Larus canus* 41cm

The common gull is not well named since it is far from being the most abundant species of gull breeding in Britain, nor is it the most numerous at any season. Adults are distinguished by having relatively slender bills, yellowish in colour, and greenish-yellow legs. They are dark eyed in contrast to their larger relations which have bright yellow eyes. In winter there are some greyish feathers on the head.

Breeding colonies are seldom large, a few pairs forming a loose community. Most British birds breed in Scotland or Ireland and while some colonies are found on beaches and small rocky islets, the majority occur inland on boggy moors or beside lochs. Juvenile birds have mottled upper parts, greyish-white heads and their light tails are marked by a broad dark band towards the tip. By the following summer they are more like their parents but still have the banded tail and the wings retain their mottling.

After breeding, there is a general movement southwards and many birds winter in England being seen on arable land, often in the company of black-headed gulls, following the plough. A variety of food is taken including worms and grubs, some vegetable material, carrion and prey disgorged by other birds after being harried. As with other gulls, they roost at night on inland and estuarine waters.

Lesser black-backed gull

Lesser Black-backed Gull *Larus fuscus* 53cm

This species is primarily a summer visitor, the majority wintering along the coastline of Portugal, southern Spain and north-west Africa. However, an increasing number now tend to remain in Britain throughout the year. Adult birds are identified by their slate-grey backs and wings, although the primaries are black, and by their bright yellow legs. In spring and autumn when Scandinavian birds are on passage they can be seen to be darker with no differentiation between the upper parts and the wing tips.

Lesser black-backed gulls breed in large and densely organised colonies on more or less level ground using the tops of cliffs, sand dunes and the plateaux of offshore islands. There are a number of inland breeding stations usually on moorland or close to lakes. The population in England and Wales exceeds that in Scotland, the largest number being on Walney Island in Lancashire. While the species is widely distributed only a few breed on the east coast south of the border.

Immature birds, during their first winter, are a darkly mottled brown, especially the upper parts, with darker primaries on the wings, a blackish bill and flesh-coloured legs. With each succeeding moult the plumage becomes more adult-like, the underparts and the head lightening, maturity being reached in the fourth summer.

As with other large gulls this species is a predator and a scavenger, being said to take more live food in the breeding season. The prey includes other birds and their eggs but also fish, shore life and earthworms obtained from arable land.

Herring Gull *Larus argentatus* 56cm

The herring gull is a resident bird which has prospered in modern times. It can now be seen almost anywhere around the coast and can be recognised by its light grey back and wings, the tips being black with white spots or 'mirrors'. A special feature is the heavy yellow bill with a red flash on the lower mandible. The legs are flesh-coloured

Herring gull nesting on bracken-covered slope

Herring gull

although some birds of this species in the Baltic and the Mediterranean have yellow legs.

Colonies of herring gulls are established on the ledges or rocky slopes of cliffs but also on flatter terraces such as shingle banks and sand dunes where they may tend to displace less vigorous species such as terns. In some parts the pressure for breeding sites is such that some birds nest on roof-tops, often becoming a nuisance due to the consequential fouling and noise, the yodelling 'kyouk-kyouk-kyouk' ringing out from dawn to dusk. They are highly successful breeders, the juveniles being very similar in appearance to those of lesser black-backed gulls.

At the end of the nesting season many herring gulls remain around the coast, some feeding on the marine life there, others haunting the fish docks taking offal and garbage. A number move inland and may frequent arable fields and rubbish dumps well away from the sea. The food obtained depends very much on local circumstances. Gulls are opportunists, a fact most evident in the breeding season when the eggs and chicks of other birds in the vicinity are consumed with great zest.

Great Black-backed Gull *Larus marinus* 74cm

This species is present at all seasons. Being the largest of the British gulls it is distinguished by its size and also by its black upper parts and pale flesh-coloured legs. As with the other larger gulls there is a heavy yellow bill bearing a red flash on the lower mandible. It flies with leisurely wing beats and, if concerned, scolds with a low pitched 'ag-ag-ag'.

Great black-backed gull

While there are some large colonies of great black-backed gulls, many birds nest either singly or in small groupings on rocky stacks or offshore islands, often close to colonies of other species on which they prey. The majority breed in Scotland but they are also present in Wales and along the rocky western and south-western shores of England. There are no regularly used sites on the east coast between the Firth of Forth and the Isle of Wight. The juveniles have mottled brown plumage but their heads and underparts are lighter than those of herring and lesser black-backed gulls. As with those species, maturity is not reached until the fourth year.

During the breeding season great black-backed gulls are voracious feeders, swallowing whole eggs, chicks and other birds such as puffins and shearwaters. They also take rabbits, shellfish and other edible material, including the offal discarded by fishing boats and at fish quays. The latter material is taken throughout the year and, in winter, rubbish dumps both at the coast and inland are visited.

Kittiwake *Rissa tridactyla* 41cm

Kittiwakes are the most oceanic of British gulls. They visit the coast to breed but when this is finished the birds leave to spend the rest of the year in northern latitudes, seldom appearing over land. An adult kittiwake is relatively lightly built with short black legs, a slender yellow bill and with black-tipped wings which lack the white 'mirrors' evident in other species. The name kittiwake comes from the oft-repeated call at the nest, 'kitti-wake, kitti-wake'.

Kittiwakes obtain their food from the sea taking floating planktonic invertebrates from the surface and also diving for plankton-feeding fish such as herring and mackerel. As with other gulls they take offal dumped overboard by fishing boats.

Breeding colonies are dense and noisy. They are situated on the steepest cliffs, the nests being compact structures cemented to the rock. During the present century the bird has enjoyed legal protection and there has been a population explosion with approximately half a million pairs now breeding in Britain and Ireland. There is great competition for suitable nesting places and some birds use window ledges or similar precarious positions not too far removed from the sea. Juveniles, which are known as 'tarrocks', are very different from those of other common British nesting gulls. In addition to a black band at the end of the light tail there is a dark collar across the back of the neck and dark wedge-shaped bands on each wing, which together form a letter 'M' running from one wing tip to the other.

Kittiwake

TERNS Family: Sternidae

Terns are more lightly built than gulls and have narrower and more acutely tapering wings. Their tails are usually forked, the points often being extended to form streamers thus giving rise to the common name 'sea swallows'. Their bills are sharply pointed and when they are fishing are held almost vertically downwards as they hover over the water. Most species obtain their food by plunge-diving in inshore waters but they rarely remain on the water swimming. As with gulls, the majority of terns are predominantly white with grey backs and black-capped heads. The black crowns or caps recede towards the end of the breeding season leaving a white forehead. All of them are summer visitors to Britain where five species breed.

Sandwich Tern *Sterna sandvicensis* 41cm

The Sandwich tern is the first of the British terns to arrive in spring, the forerunners appearing towards the end of March. Apart from its size it is distinguished by its black legs and bill, the latter ending in a sharp yellow tip, and a tail which is not deeply forked. In the air it calls with a rasping 'kirrick'. On the ground the elongated feathers at the back of the crown often project giving a crest-like effect and the whiteness on the forehead which is a feature of winter plumage is evident as early as June in some individuals.

Sandwich tern

Sandwich terns nest in tightly-packed colonies on shingle beaches, sandy dunes and islands, often in close association with black-headed gulls or other terns. They are somewhat volatile and unpredictable, disturbance of a nesting colony sometimes resulting in the whole assembly moving off to fresh quarters leaving behind deserted nests and broken eggs. The largest concentrations occur along the east coast, particularly in Northumberland and Norfolk. Orkney represents their most northerly breeding station.

A special feature of this species is the way in which the young are tended. In some colonies at about two weeks old they are led to the shore and formed up into parties which then move around near the water's edge in compact groups. They are fed on small fish, especially sand eels, obtained from rather deeper water than that used by other terns. The juveniles can fly when about five weeks old. At this stage their upper parts are mottled with brown. Initially they move along the coast seeking places where food is plentiful, but by August or September both adults and young are ready to start their autumnal migration to West and South African waters.

Common Tern *Sterna hirundo* 36cm
Common terns arrive on the south coast during April and proceed northwards along the eastern and western seaboards so that during the summer they may be seen in suitable undisturbed habitats as far north as the Shetlands. They are distinguished from other similar sized terns by their bills which are scarlet or orange-red and tipped with black. In the air, and viewed from below, the inner four primary flight feathers are lighter and more translucent than the outer ones thus creating a distinctive pattern. When breeding, the arrival of an intruder elicits an agitated response with birds rising and sweeping down repeatedly, each dive being accompanied by a chattering 'kee-yaah'.

Terneries are established on sand dunes, sand or shingle banks and low-lying islands, the nests usually being more widely separated than those of Sandwich terns. Sometimes common terns nest inland on similar sites associated with flooded gravel pits or more natural lakes. At some nature reserves artificial breeding platforms or rafts are readily taken over. The chicks are fed by the parents in the main on small fish obtained close inshore. The mantles and heads of juvenile birds are tinted gingery brown and another distinguishing feature is

Common tern

the dark band along the upper margin of the folded wing.

By the end of July terneries are being deserted and during August and September most birds are migrating southwards so as to winter in tropical conditions along the coast of Africa as far down as the Cape.

Arctic Tern *Sterna paradisaea* 41cm

Arctic terns are similar in appearance to common terns, the two species often being referred to collectively as 'comic terns'. They differ in small details. In summer an Arctic tern's red bill lacks a black tip, its red legs are shorter and the plumage is more dusky. Both species have forked tails but the streamers of the Arctic are longer and project beyond the tips of the closed wings. In the air, viewed against the light, an Arctic tern's primaries all seem to be translucent. The call note, 'kee-yaah', resembles that of the common tern but the emphasis is on the second syllable rather than the first. In juvenile birds the plumage is rather lighter in tone, the dark marking on the

Arctic tern

folded wing is less distinct and the gingery tint is missing from the whitish forehead.

Common terns and Arctic terns are sometimes found nesting together in colonies close to the coast. At the same time their ranges differ to an appreciable extent. The common tern does not breed much further north than the Shetlands whereas the Arctic is found on shores and islands fringing the Polar basin. In Britain the Arctic tern's more northerly distribution is reflected in the fact that apart from Northumberland, Cumbria and Anglesey only a very few pairs nest around the coastline of England and Wales. Nevertheless its abundance in Scotland is such that it is by far the most numerous of British terns.

Colonies of Arctic terns are noisy assemblies. However, on occasion, and for no apparent reason, there is a pause in the clamour and the birds take off in silence, sweeping over the sea before returning to their nests. This eerie performance is referred to as a 'dread'.

Arctic terns cover considerable distances on migration. Although many spend the summer in the far north they may winter about the shores of the Antarctic continent. The round trip may involve a journey of approximately 20,000 miles.

Roseate Tern *Sterna dougallii* 38cm

The roseate tern is so named because of the delicate rosy flush present on the breast and belly for a short time in spring. At a distance the upper parts are a paler grey and the underparts whiter than in the similar sized common and Arctic terns. The bill is largely black and the tail streamers are very long, projecting well beyond the wing tips when at rest on the ground. In flight the wing beats are shallower than those of other terns and the call note is a rasping 'kaak'.

Roseate terns are the last of the migrant terns to arrive in spring and they are the least common. There are relatively few sites in Britain and Ireland which are used regularly and these are all coastal. The most

Roseate tern

heavily populated colonies are in Ireland. From time to time one or two pairs will settle down alongside established groups of other terns but such nesting is sporadic. In the company of common or Arctic terns the juveniles have more heavily mottled upper parts and their legs and bills are black.

British and Irish roseate terns winter along the West African coast. As with 'comic' terns, immature birds remain in southern waters during their first summer, migrating northwards in the second year although, in fact, most will not breed before they are three years old.

Little Tern *Sterna albifrons* 23cm

The little tern is not much more than half the size of the other British nesting terns and differs from them in spring by having a white forehead bounded on each side by a black eyestripe running to the base of the bill. The colour of the very slender bill is yellow tipped with black and the legs are also yellow. In the air its wings move faster than those of its larger relatives and when it is fishing it hovers over the water on flickering wing-beats. Most of its food is caught in shallow creeks or close inshore. A high-pitched 'kik-kik' is its usual call note while a more excited 'kirri-kirri' is used during display flights over the breeding grounds.

Little terns nest on flat sandy and shingle beaches. The simple shallow nesting scrapes are usually widely separated, in the open and often situated close to the high water mark. Consequently they may be washed out by tidal surges. In addition beaches of this type are favoured by holidaymakers and, as a result, the availability of suitable nesting sites has been reduced considerably during the present century. It is not surprising that the little tern competes with the roseate tern for the status of being the rarest of Britain's coastal nesting terns. It is most numerous on the flatter east coast of England south of the Humber and also along the southern seaboard.

After breeding the black crown of the adult recedes and the forward arm of the dark eyestripe is lost. The juveniles are similarly patterned but their legs and bills are duller and their backs are marked with brown 'horseshoes'. All move south in the autumn to spend the winter months off the coast of Africa.

Opposite, little tern

AUKS Family: Alcidae

Auks are medium-sized, stockily-built seabirds which are mainly black and white in colour. They are confined to the northern hemisphere, occupying a similar niche to the penguins in the southern hemisphere. Except when they are breeding, they spend all their time at sea. They are expert divers, using their short sturdy wings when submerged for propulsion. The laterally-compressed bill, frequently specially ornamented, is used to secure fish and other marine creatures.

Since the wings are relatively small they must beat rapidly to keep the body airborne. Sustained flight is unusual, shorter flights being rapid and direct, and on coming in to land there is no gentle approach, the broad webbed feet being held outstretched initially to reduce speed and later to absorb the shock of impact. On land auks adopt an erect posture since, as with other divers, the legs are set well back. Many shuffle along with the whole of the foot pressed close to the ground, puffins being rather more mobile. They are gregarious birds often nesting in huge colonies.

Guillemot *Uria aalge* 42cm

This is probably the most numerous of the seabirds breeding around the coastline of Britain and Ireland. Adults in summer dress have their heads and upper parts chocolate-brown with white underneath. In contrast to other auks the relatively small head, bearing a slender pointed bill, is borne on a slim sinuous neck. But there is more than one race and the description applies to the southern race, the range of which extends into southern Scotland.

Further north, birds have upper parts which are black in colour rather than chocolate-brown. There is another variation. Some birds have a white ring round the eye with a white line running backwards across the head. This is the 'bridled' form and on the south coast 'bridled' birds make up about one per cent of the population, the percentage increasing on moving northwards until a figure of approximately twenty-five per cent applies in Scotland.

Guillemots breed in enormous numbers on the flat and narrow ledges of steep cliffs, each available space being packed with birds standing shoulder to shoulder, their snaky heads bowing and stretching to the accompaniment of a raucous chorus. A single egg is

Opposite, guillemot

laid on the bare rock. It is pyriform in shape, tending to spin rather than roll, thus minimising the chance of being lost over the edge. The young are fed on small fish and leave their ledges at a comparatively early age. After three weeks the plumage is complete and waterproof. They cannot fly but around this time they flutter down to the sea, usually in the evening, and in the company of adults swim away from the vicinity of the colony under the cover of darkness.

In winter plumage the adult has the throat and the sides of the head coloured white. At this time it is at sea.

Razorbill *Alca torda* 41cm

The razorbill is so named because of the shape of its beak which, during the summer, is handsomely marked in black and white. It is well suited for grasping fish and other marine animals. When seen in association with the much more numerous guillemot the larger head and stouter neck of the razorbill is very evident.

Razorbills breed on cliffs or rocky stacks usually laying their eggs out of sight beneath boulders, in sheltered corners or within deep crevices. Their colonies are diffuse, they do not stand in close formations like guillemots. At the same time their breeding biology is similar. Single egg clutches are laid and young birds flutter down to the water on wings whose flight feathers are not yet fully developed. They are barely three weeks old and move away from the colony to the open sea. Even at this stage they swim and dive freely.

After breeding razorbills disperse to spend the autumn and winter at sea. In winter dress the breast and throat are white, the bill rather smaller and unmarked. During January and February birds begin to assemble in groups on the sea beneath their breeding stations. Initially they are present for short periods in the mornings. Sitting on the water they appear plump and compact holding their bills and tails stiffly erect. They indulge in complex displays. Pairs swim around each other with mouths open showing their yellow interiors while uttering guttural cries. Groups swim in line ahead before there is a mass dive followed by birds chasing each other erratically below the surface. In due course the breeding sites are occupied and eggs laid, usually in May.

Opposite, razorbill

Black Guillemot *Cepphus grylle* 34cm

The black guillemot, which is often referred to by the old Norse name 'tystie', is much less abundant than the common guillemot. It does not form massed colonies, pairs nesting singly or in small groups on rocky or boulder-strewn shores usually not far above the high water mark. In contrast to the other auks two eggs are laid and they are hidden under fallen slabs of rock or in almost inaccessible crevices. Probably because they are relatively safe from predators the young do not take

Black guillemot

to the water until they are fully fledged, by which time they are about five weeks old.

In nuptial dress black guillemots are sooty black with contrasting white wing patches and red feet. They are most often seen floating on the water not far from the shore. A complete change occurs in the autumn, the birds then being mottled grey above with white underparts. The conspicuous white wing patches are retained along with the black flight feathers. Juveniles are not unlike the adults in winter dress except that the wing patches are not pure white.

In Britain this species is at the southern limit of distribution. On the west coast it reaches as far south as Anglesey but on the east there are no breeding sites south of the Moray Firth. The birds finish nesting in July. They do not undertake lengthy migratory journeys and since they tend to feed in shallow waters most of them winter around the coast not far from their breeding quarters.

Puffin *Fratercula arctica* 30cm

Puffins have the usual black and white plumage of the auks but are at once distinguished by the striking triangular, parrot-like, multi-coloured bill and the orange-red legs and feet. On closer examination there are other facial adornments: blue-grey horny patches above and below the eye and yellow wattles at the angles of the jaws. On land only the webbed toes are placed flat on the ground and they walk and jump more effectively than guillemots and razorbills.

Puffins appear to winter further out to sea than other auks and are later returning to their breeding stations, arriving no earlier than mid-March. Nesting puffins favour grassy slopes at the tops of cliffs or on low-lying islands. Here burrows are excavated a metre or more in length. For this work the bill is used as a pickaxe and the webbed feet as shovels. Since puffins are extremely sociable birds and colonies may number thousands, a whole area may be tunnelled and undermined so that the site after some years may become unsafe and untenable. A single egg is laid and there is a long incubation period of about six weeks after which the chick is fed in the burrow, mainly on small fish, for a further six weeks until it is fully fledged. Feeding now stops and the juvenile slims down before emerging at night to stumble and flutter to the sea. This first excursion is made in darkness to minimise the chance of attack by predatory gulls.

After breeding the adults lose much of their colouring. The wattles and eye patches disappear, the bill is less colourful and the whole face becomes dusky. Juveniles are somewhat browner and the bill is more slender and dark. Colonies are deserted during August. The birds move out to sea and the young will not return for two or three years.

Puffin

PASSERINES Order: Passeriformes

Passerine birds are characterised by having feet with three toes pointing forwards and one backwards, an arrangement facilitating perching. They have other anatomical features in common and the group includes all the small songbirds.

Many passerines make an appearance at the coast. Some are on migration, some are making forays for food but a few breed near the shore while others make the coast their headquarters for an appreciable part of the year.

Shore Lark *Eremophila alpestris* 16cm

Shore larks winter on the east coast and especially on East Anglian shores. They are visitors from northern Scandinavia and Russia and may be seen fluttering over shingle banks and saltings looking for

Shore larks in summer

seeds shed at the end of the summer by strand plants. In addition they search for food amongst the seaweed and litter which accumulates at the high tide mark. Slightly smaller than skylarks, their plumage is lighter in colour and less heavily streaked, dark markings being almost absent from the breast in the adult. At close quarters the black gorget and the patterned head, horned in the male, are distinctive although in winter these features are rather muted.

Rock Pipit *Anthus spinoletta* 16cm

In summer, rock pipits are restricted to rocky shores. Nests are hidden in clefts or in recesses among the turfy mounds covering cliff ledges. If disturbed they flit from one rocky perch to another uttering a sad monosyllabic 'tseep'. When nesting is over they disperse and some birds forsake their usual environment spending the winter on salt marshes and muddy shores.

The rock pipit spends much of its time exploring tidal litter hunting for flies which hatch from rotting seaweed and also for sandhoppers. In general it is more dusky than pipits and larks, dark olive-brown above with paler underparts, darkly flecked. The legs are almost black and the outer tail feathers lack the pure whiteness evident in the skylark and meadow pipit.

Rock pipit

Twite

Twite *Carduelis flavirostris* 13cm

Twites breed in upland areas but parties spend the winter at the coast feeding on the seeds available from shingle ridge and salt marsh plants. A close relation of the linnet, it is distinguished from that species by an unmarked orange-buff throat with some darker streaks appearing on the sides of the breast and belly. The bill is yellow, much lighter than a linnet's, and while there is no red on the breast and crown, pinkness is evident on the rump. The call note is a nasal 'twa-eet'.

Snow Bunting *Plectrophenax nivalis* 17cm

A very small number of this species breeds in Scotland but the majority of those which winter in Britain come from the far north, the snow bunting being the most northerly breeding passerine. It nests in barren rocky areas bordering the coasts of both the Old and New Worlds around the Polar basin.

Snow buntings are much commoner on the east coast than the west. In breeding plumage the males are largely white with black backs and with the wings and tails darkly tipped. Flocks in the air do, indeed, resemble snowflakes. During the winter months the whiteness is tinged with buff and the darkness of the back is relieved by greyish-brown streaks. The feathering of the hen birds at all times is similar to that of the cocks in winter dress.

Snow buntings are restless birds flitting above the tide-line over shingle banks and sandy dunes searching for the seeds which make up their winter diet.

Snow bunting male in summer plumage